The Treasury of C..... ....ildren

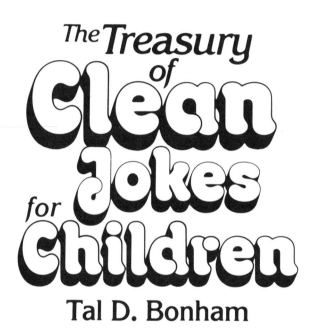

The Treasury of Clean Jokes for Children

Tal D. Bonham

Broadman Press
Nashville, Tennessee

4257-21
ISBN: 0-8054-5721-6

Dewey Decimal Classification: J808.87
Subject Heading: JOKES

Library of Congress Catalog Card Number: 87-6329
Printed in the United States of America

Library of Congress Cataloging-in-Publication Data

Bonham, Tal D., 1934-
 The treasury of clean jokes for children.

 Summary: Provides jokes in such categories as brain
teasers, school jokes, silly questions, animal jokes,
and brother and sister jokes.
 1. American wit and humor. 2. Wit and humor,
Juvenile. [1. Jokes] I. Title.
PN6163.B66 1987   818'.5402   87-6329
ISBN 0-8054-5721-6 (pbk.)

To Heather Nicole
her mother, Marilyn
and
her three funny uncles
Randy, Danny, and Tal David

Acknowledgments

Thank you Mr. and Mrs. Charles Tommey for helping to put it all together . . . and thank you, Faye, (the grandmother of my grandchild) for all you have done to help . . . and thank you Esther, Doris, Tina, Lana, and Pam for your help and good ideas. A very special word of thanks for Janet Tommey who acted as our resident critic and provided much of the material for the book.

Preface

Several years ago, I put together a clean joke book and my friends said, "Do another one!"

We did another one and teenagers said, "Do one just for us!"

We did a joke book just for teenagers and businessmen said, "Do a book of clean business jokes!"

We did a book of business jokes and sports fans said, "It's time for a sports joke book."

After I finished the sports joke book, ministers called for a good book of church jokes.

Then came a book of country jokes. That makes seven clean joke books in all.

Count em' 1-2-3-4-5-6-7.

But you know what? They tell me that children are some of the biggest readers of my seven joke books.

Many parents and kids have said, "Now,

why don't you do a joke book just for the children?"

Well, here it is! It contains those special kinds of jokes just for kids. I hope you enjoy them.

TAL D. BONHAM

Contents

Knock! Knock!
Who's there?
Sarah,
Sarah, who?
Sarah doorbell around here? I'm tired of knocking!

Yes! There is a doorbell around here. If you are tired of knocking, ring the doorbell for a change. Turn the page for the world's first Ding-a-ling jokes!

Ding-a-ling Jokes

Ding-a-ling!
Who's there?
Hugo.
Hugo who?
Hugo to the head of the class!

Ding-a-ling!
Who's there?
Display.
Display who?
Dis play, dat's work.

Ding-a-ling!
Who's there?
Jimmy.
Jimmy who?
Jimmy a little kiss, will ya, huh?

Ding-a-ling!
Who's there?
Dos.
Dos who?
Dos debug byte?

Ding-a-ling!
Who's there?
Butternut.
Butternut who?
Butternut let me in. My feet are muddy.

Ding-a-ling!
Who's there?
Digital.
Digital who?
Digital your programmer you wanted a printout?

Ding-a-ling!
Who's there?
Boo.
Boo who?
Don't cry, little baby.

Ding-a-ling!
Who's there?
Hardware.
Hardware who?
Hard where you run up a hill, easy where you run down.

Ding-a-ling!
Who's there?
Dewey.
Dewey who?
Dewey have to go to school today?

Ding-a-ling!
Who's there?
Bug.
Bug who?
Anyone bug me!

Ding-a-ling!
Who's there?
Accordion.
Accordion who?
Accordion to the paper, it's gonna rain to-night.

Ding-a-ling!
Who's there?
Canoe.
Canoe who?
Canoe come out and play with me?

Ding-a-ling!
Who's there?
Boyd.
Boyd who?
Boy, do you ask a lot of questions!

Ding-a-ling!
Who's there?
Cargo.
Cargo who?
Cargo beep beep.

Ding-a-ling!
Who's there?
Major.
Major who?
Major open the door, didn't I?

Ding-a-ling!
Who's there?
Howie.
Howie who?
I'm fine, how are you?

Ding-a-ling!
Who's there?
Sam.
Sam who?
Sam times you make me so mad!

Ding-a-ling!
Who's there?
Sarah.
Sarah who?
Sarah fly on your nose, or is that just a freckle?

Ding-a-ling!
Who's there?
Yule.
Yule who?
Yule never know how much I love you.

Ding-a-ling!
Who's there?
Ira.
Ira who?
Ira member, why can't you?

Ding-a-ling!
Who's there?
Scold.
Scold who?
Scold outside, let me in!

Ding-a-ling!
Who's there?
Little old lady.
Little old lady who?
I didn't know that you could yodel.

Ding-a-ling!
Who's there?
Gwen.
Gwen who?
Gwen my way?

Ding-a-ling!
Who's there?
Ben.
Ben who?
Ben over and get the note I dropped.

Ding-a-ling!
Who's there?
Halibut.
Halibut who?
Halibut letting me borrow a dollar?

Ding-a-ling!
Who's there?
Shirley.
Shirley who?
Shirley you didn't forget your lunch money again.

Ding-a-ling!
Who's there?
Handsome.
Handsome who?
Handsome pizza to me, please.

Ding-a-ling!
Who's there?
Iowa.
Iowa who?
Iowa quarter to the library, Mom.

Ding-a-ling!
Who's there?
The force.
The force who?
The force time I rang, nobody answered!

Ding-a-ling!
Who's there?
Wanda.
Wanda who?
Wanda play with me after school?

Ding-a-ling!
Who's there?
Isabelle.
Isabelle who?
Isabelle ringing? I thought I heard one.

Ding-a-ling!
Who's there?
Lena.
Lena who?
Lena little closer, and I'll whisper in your ear.

Ding-a-ling!
Who's there?
Jamaica.
Jamaica who?
Jamaica passing grade in math?

Ding-a-ling!
Who's there?
Henny.
Henny who?
Henny body wanna jump rope?

Ding-a-ling!
Who's there?
Dwayne.
Dwayne who?
Dwayne the bathtub. I'm dwowning.

Ding-a-ling!
Who's there?
Rita.
Rita who?
Rita book and you might learn something.

Ding-a-ling!
Who's there?
Lil.
Lil who?
Lil things mean a lot.

Ding-a-ling!
JANE: Will you remember me in five years?
DICK: Yes.
JANE: Will you remember me in ten years?
DICK: Yes.
JANE: Will you remember me in twenty years?

DICK: Yes.
JANE: Ding-a-ling!
DICK: Who's there?
JANE: See, you forgot me already!

Ding-a-ling!
Who's there?
Rocky.
Rocky who?
Rocky-bye baby, in the treetop.

Ding-a-ling!
Who's there?
Rhoda.
Rhoda who?
Rhoda bicycle yesterday and fell off.

Ding-a-ling!
Who's there?
O'Shea.
O'Shea who?
O'Shea can you shee by the dawn's early light?

Ding-a-ling!
Who's there?
Heidi
Heidi who?
Heidi-n here, they'll never find us!

Ding-a-ling!
Who's there?
Sarah.
Sarah who?
Sarah doctor in the house?

Ding-a-ling!
Who's there?
Wade.
Wade who?
Wade and see!

Ding-a-ling!
Who's there?
Watson.
Watson who?
Not much. Watson who with you?

Ding-a-ling!
Who's there?
Ella.
Ella who?
Ella-mentary school is the pits.

Ding-a-ling!
Who's there?
Wayne.
Wayne who?
Waynedwops keep falling on my head.

Ding-a-ling!
Who's there?
Ida.
Ida who?
Ida wanna tell you.

Ding-a-ling!
Who's there?
Banana.
Ding-a-ling!
Who's there?
Banana.
Ding-a-ling!
Who's there?
Banana.
Ding-a-ling!
Who's there?
Orange.
Orange who?
Orange you glad I didn't say banana
again?

Ding-a-ling!
Who's there?
Yukon.
Yukon, who?
Yukon lead a horse to water, but you can't make it drink!

Ding-a-ling!
Who's there?
Thesis.
Thesis who?
Thesis . . . a recording.

Ding-a-ling!
Who's there?
Owl.
Owl who?
Owl never tell.

Ding-a-ling!
Who's there?
Murray.
Murray who?
Murray Christmas to all.

Ding-a-ling!
Who's there?
Pizza.
Pizza who?
Pizza on earth, goodwill to men.

Ding-a-ling!
Who's there?
Who.
Who who?
What are you, an owl?

Ding-a-ling!
Who's there?
Gopher.
Gopher who?
Gopher a long walk and don't come back!

Ding-a-ling!
Who's there?
Eaton.
Eaton who?
Eaton between meals is a no-no!

Ding-a-ling!
Who's there?
Dishes.
Dishes who?
Dishes the FBI, open up!

Ding-a-ling!
Who's there?
Abie.
Abie who?
Abie cdefg.

Ding-a-ling!
Who's there?
Pecan.
Pecan who?
Pecan someone your own size!

Ding-a-ling!
Who's there?
Sol.
Sol who?
Sol-long, it's been good to know you.

Ding-a-ling!
Who's there?
Authur.
Authur who?
Arthur any more at home like you?

Ding-a-ling!
Who's there?
Les.
Les who?
Les stop doing ding-a-lings!

Ding-a-ling!
Who's there?
Thad.
Thad who?
Thad's all, folks!

Children's Capers

DANNY: What are you doing, Sis?
MARILYN: Writing my cousin a letter.
DANNY: Why are you writing so slow?
MARILYN: Because he can't read very fast.

"Brian!" shouted his mother. "There were two pieces of chocolate cake in the pantry last night and now there's only one. How do you explain that?"

"It was dark in the pantry, Mother," said Brian. "I didn't see the other piece."

"Hello, Janet," said Martha. "Do you like your school?"

"Sometimes," she answered.

"When is that?" Martha asked.

"When it's closed," Janet replied.

DAVID: Dad, that dentist wasn't painless like he advertised.

FATHER: Did he hurt you, Son?

DAVID: No, but did he scream when I bit his finger!

MOM: T. D., how can you practice your trumpet and listen to the radio at the same time?

T. D.: I have two ears.

A father brought his boss home for dinner. The whole family was seated around the dining table as the father carved the roast beef.

The son looked down at the beef on his plate and said, "This is the funniest looking drumstick I ever saw!"

"That's beef," replied the mother. "What made you think it was a drumstick?"

"This morning before Dad went to work, he said he was bringing some turkey home for dinner!"

"Why are you crying, Billy?"

"Because my new tennis shoes hurt."

"That's because you put them on the wrong feet."

"Well, they're the only feet I have."

MOTHER: Sara, haven't you finished filling the salt shaker yet?

SARA: Not yet, Mom. It's awful hard to get the salt through those little holes!"

ABIGAIL: I won 186 goldfish.

STACY: Where do you keep them?

ABIGAIL: In the bathroom.

STACY: What do you do when you want to take a bath?

ABIGAIL: I blindfold them.

Randy was having his eyes examined. "Have your eyes been checked before?" asked the doctor.

"As far as I know," Randy replied, "they've always been solid brown."

"Mrs. Johnston, your daughter would be a fine dancer except for two things."

"What are they?"

"Her feet!"

"Mom," Jimmy yelled from the kitchen, "You know that dish you were always worried I'd break?"

"Yes dear, what about it?"

"Well, your worries are over."

AMY: I'm so glad I'm not a bird.
FATHER: Why?
AMY: I can't fly!

STEVE: Boy! was I ever in hot water last night.
MARY: You were? What did you do?
STEVE: I took a bath.

MOTHER: Don't be selfish. Let your brother use the sled half the time.
SON: I do, Mom. I use it going down the hill, and he gets to use it coming up.

Little Nathan fell off his bicycle and cut his knee. His mother bathed and dressed the wound, and then gave the boy a pill to soothe him.

After he swallowed it, Nathan asked, "How will the pill know which leg to go down?"

MOTHER: Patrick, if you don't stop banging that drum I'll go out of my mind!

PATRICK: Too late, Mom. I stopped an hour ago.

SIX-YEAR-OLD BOY: I'd buy that dog, but his legs are too short.

CLERK: Too short? Why, all four of them touch the floor.

Scott was applying for a summer job.

"How old are you, Son?" asked the owner of the shop.

"I'm twelve years old, Sir," answered Scott.

"And what do you expect to be when you grow up?"

"Twenty-one, Sir."

FATHER: Where's this morning's newspaper?

SON: I wrapped the garbage in it and threw it out.

FATHER: I wanted to see it.

SON: There wasn't much to see. Only an apple core, two steak bones, and some coffee grounds.

FATHER: Doctor, come quick! My boy just swallowed our pocket-size TV!

DOCTOR: I'll be right over. What are you doing in the meantime?

FATHER: I don't know. I guess we'll have to listen to the radio.

It was getting close to Christmas and the mother asked her ten-year-old daughter, "What would you like to get as a gift?"

"A mirror, Mommy," came the reply.

"My goodness. Why?"

"Because," sighed the daughter, "I'm getting to big to make up in the doorknob."

"Mike, I hear you've been fighting with one of those boys next door and have given him a black eye."

"Yes'm. You see, they're twins and I wanted some way to tell them apart."

Two young boys were folding paper airplanes. "What kind of paper makes the best planes?" asked one boy.

"Fly paper," replied the other boy.

A ten-year-old went into a costume shop and said, "I'm going to a Halloween party and I'd like to rent a costume. What have you got?"

"How about a pirate costume?" suggested the owner. "I can give you a knit cap, a silk shirt, satin pants, leather boots, and a real sword for $50."

"I didn't want to spend that much. You got anything cheaper?"

"You can have the cap, a sweatshirt, plain pants, boots, and a rubber sword for $25."

"That's still too expensive," complained the child.

"How about the cap, pants, sneakers and a cardboard sword for $10?" asked the owner.

"No, that's still too high."

"Well then, for $5 I can give you a broomstick and a can of red spray paint."

"What can I do with that?" asked the child.

"Put the broomstick in your mouth, spray the paint on your head, and go as a candy apple!"

KAREN: Have you noticed that Daddy is getting taller?

KEITH: No, why?

KAREN: His head is sticking through his hair.

Little Rusty stood in a department store near the escalator watching the moving handrail.

"Something wrong, Son?" inquired the security guard.

"Nope," replied the boy, "just waiting for my chewing gum to come back."

JACK: What's the difference between a cake and a school bus?

JIM: I don't know.

JACK: I'm glad I didn't send you to pick up my birthday cake.

"Can you lend me $1,000?"

"I only have $800."

"That is all right, you can owe me the other $200."

JOHN: I'm going to cross a galaxy with a frog.

SHARON: You'd better not. You'll be sorry.

JOHN: Why?

SHARON: Don't you know what you'll get?

JOHN: No. What?

SHARON: Star warts.

MOTHER: Jared, get your little sister's hat out of that puddle.

JARED: I can't, Mom, she's got it strapped too tight under her chin.

BOY: What does your Dad sell?

GIRL: Salt.

BOY: Well, my dad is a salt seller too.

GIRL: Shake.

DAN: If you eat any more ice cream, you'll burst.

MONTY: OK. Pass the ice cream and duck.

Karen wanted to be a doctor when she grew up. She bandaged and cared for her dolls, and often went on imaginary sick calls to someone in the neighborhood.

One day she ran out on such a call, forgetting to close the door behind her. When her mother insisted she come back and shut it, Karen did so and raced away.

That evening her mother asked, "How is the patient getting along?"

"She died," said Karen. "Died while I was closing that door!"

KATHY: Glenn, Mom says to run across the street and see how old Mrs. Planter is.

GLENN: OK.

MOM (to *Glenn*): Well, what did she say?

GLENN: She says it's none of your business how old she is.

BENJAMIN: Mother, please change my name.

MOTHER: But why should I do that?

BENJAMIN: Because Dad says he's going to spank me as sure as my name's Benjamin.

A six-year-old was sent to Sunday School with this note pinned to her coat: "The opinions expressed by this child concerning God and the Bible may not necessarily be those of her family."

DAD: Son, why is your January report card so bad?

SON: You know how it is, Dad. Things are always marked down after Christmas.

Chris had his backpack ready to leave for camp.

"Did you remember to put in some toothpaste?" asked his mother.

"I don't expect to get in a fight," said Chris, "and my teeth aren't loose."

KEITH: I bet I can make you say "black." What are the colors of the flag?

MOTHER: Red, white and blue.

KEITH: I told you that I could make you say "black."

MOTHER: I didn't say "black."

PENNY: Will you join me in a cup of hot chocolate?

MINDY: Yes, but do you think we'll both fit?

"Mother, I just took a splinter out of my hand with a pin."

"A pin! Don't you know that's dangerous?"

"Oh, no, Mother, I used a safety pin."

"Your cat has been staring at that yard light," said Kerrie. "Is he all right?"

"Oh," said Misty. "He's trying to make a moth bawl."

"What's wrong, Son?" asked Mark's father.

"I lost my puppy," sobbed Mark.

"Don't cry," said the concerned father. "We'll get your dog back. "We'll put an ad in the paper."

"That won't do any good," wailed Mark. "The dog can't read!"

"Come see my new kittens," said Laura.

"How cute," said Cindy, watching them play. "Will you have to get your cats a license?"

"Of course not," said Laura. "They don't know how to drive!"

ROBBIE: May I have a quarter for the crying man outside?

MOTHER: What crying man?

ROBBIE: The one that's crying, "Ice cream! Ice cream!"

JAMES: Did you find your cat?

PETE: Yes, he was in the refrigerator.

JAMES: Goodness, is he OK?

PETE: He's more than OK; he's a cool cat.

The second grader was in bed with a cold and a high temperature.

"How high is it, Doctor?" he wanted to know.

"One hundred and three, Son," said the doctor.

"What is the world's record?"

CINDY: My kitten likes to drink lemonade.

KIM: Boy, he sure must be a sourpuss.

BOY: How much is a soft drink?

WAITRESS: Fifty cents.

BOY: How much is a refill?

WAITRESS: The first is free.

BOY: Well, then, I'll have a refill.

A girl rushed into the doctor's office and said: "Doctor, I think I'm going crazy. I have a carrot growing out of my left ear."

"So you have," said the amazed doctor. "How can such a thing happen?"

"I can't understand it," said the bewildered girl. "I planted cabbage."

Jason and Nathan were quarreling about whose father was the stronger.

JASON: Well, you know the Pacific Ocean? My father's the one who dug the hole for it.

NATHAN: Ah, that's nothing. You know the Dead Sea? My father's the one who killed it.

TREVOR: That's a cool pair of stockings you have on, Jill. One red and one green.

JILL: Yes, and I have another pair just like it at home.

Crisscross Jokes

What do you get when you cross a frog with a chair?
A toadstool.

What do you get when you cross a rooster and a bell?
An alarm cluck.

What do you get when you cross a cat with a laughing hyena?
A gigglepuss!

What do you get when you cross a cow and a pogo stick?
A milkshaker.

What do you get when you cross a monster with a computer?
A 500-pound genius.

What do you get when you cross a worm and a fur coat?

A caterpillar.

"I crossed a cow with a kangaroo."

"What did you get?"

"I'm not sure, but you have to milk it on a pogo stick."

What do you get when you cross two cherry pies and handlebars?

A pie-cycle.

What do you get when you cross a porcupine with a gorilla?

Any seat you want on the school bus.

What do you get when you cross a cactus and a porcupine?

Sore hands.

What do you get if you cross a turkey with an ostrich?

A Thanksgiving bird that buries its head in the dressing.

What do you get when you cross an octopus with a mink?

A fur coat with lots of sleeves.

What do you get when you cross a whale with a penguin?

A submarine in a tuxedo.

What do you get when you cross a computer with a gorilla?

A hairy reasoner.

What do you get when you cross a computer with a refrigerator?

Very cool answers.

What do you get when you cross a peanut with a porcupine?

Stickers in your peanut butter.

What do you get when you cross a prune with a peach?

A fruit that's really the pits!

What do you get when you cross a walnut with a banana?

I don't know, but it would sure be hard to peel.

What do you get when you cross a computer with a blender?

A mixed solution.

What do you get when you cross a hiker with a little gossip?

A walkie-talkie.

What do you get when you cross a bee with a bell?

A humdinger.

What do you get when you cross a computer with an alligator?

Either snappy answers or a computer with a byte.

What do you get when you cross a camel with the town dump?

Humpty-Dumpty.

What do you get when you cross a polyester suit with a wolf?

A wash-and wear wolf.

What do you get when you cross a lion with a peacock?

A dandelion.

What do you get when you cross a computer with an elephant?

A five-ton know-it-all.

What do you get when you cross a computer with a rabbit?

A computer that jumps to conclusions.

What do you get when you cross a kangaroo with a mink?

A fur jumper with pockets.

What do you get when you cross a computer with a mule?

A computer that gives you a real kick when you plug it in.

What do you get when you cross a porcupine with a worm?

Barbed wire.

What did everyone say when the science teacher crossed a computer with a skunk?

C P U !

What do you get when you cross peanut butter with an elephant?

You either get peanut butter that never forgets or an elephant that sticks to the roof of your mouth.

If a fat cat is a flabby tabby, what's a very small cat?

An itty-bitty kitty!

Brain Teasers

Problem: How can you throw a baseball with all your might and, without hitting a wall, car, or anything else, have it stop and come right back to you?

Solution: Throw it up in the air right over your head.

Six copy cats are sitting on a fence. If one jumps off, how many are left?

None. The others follow.

Problem: A man who lived out in the country had to walk home one day carrying a fox, a goose, and a bag of corn. He took a shortcut through the woods and had to cross a river to get home. There was a boat big enough for him to cross the river with only one possession at a time. If he left the goose and the corn together, the goose would eat the corn. If he left the goose and the fox together, the fox would eat the goose. How did the man get all three safely across the river?

Solution: First he took the goose across the river. Then he took the fox across the river and brought the goose back. Next he took the corn across, leaving the goose. Finally, he returned alone and brought the goose across.

What do you have when you have three big ducks, four little ducks, and two medium-size ducks?
A box of quackers.

What do you use to see through a wall?
A window.

Problem: You are flying a plane that travels from Columbus, Ohio, to Oklahoma City—a distance of 600 air miles. The plane goes 200 miles an hour, and it makes one stop for 30 minutes. What is the pilot's name?
Solution: Whatever your name is.

If two is company, and three is a crowd, what are four and five?

Nine.

If a feather weighs two ounces, and a half box of feathers weighs one pound, how much will three pounds of feathers weigh?

Three pounds.

April showers bring May flowers. Then what do May flowers bring?

June bugs.

What did the mama broom and the papa broom say to the baby broom?

"Go to sweep."

A farmer was asked how many cows he had. He said, "When they are in line there are two cows ahead of a cow, two cows behind a cow, and one in the middle." How many cows did he have?

Three.

What four letters of the alphabet would frighten a thief?

O I C U.

How do you divide thirteen apples among nineteen people?

Make applesauce.

Problem: Billy wants to stand behind George and George wants to stand behind Billy. How would you arrange that?

Solution: Let them stand back to back.

Question: There is an English word with four letters. It reads the same when you look at it forward, backward, or upside down, if it is printed in capital letters. What is the word?

Answer: NOON.

I never ask any questions, but I get a great many answers. What am I?

A doorbell.

A butcher is six-feet two-inches tall and wears a size eleven and a-half shoe. What does he weigh?

Meat, of course.

Problem: In how many states is it legal for a man to marry his widow's sister?

Solution: None. Only dead men have widows.

What animal is it which walks first on four legs, later on two, and in old age on three?

A person.

How many wheelbarrows of dirt can you take out of a hole two feet square and two feet deep?

None. The dirt has already been removed from a hole.

How many lions can you put into an empty cage?

One—then it would not be empty.

Problem: A father has two sons, Dan and Dave. The man weighs 200 pounds. Dan and Dave each weigh 100 pounds. They want to cross a river in a boat that can only carry 200 pounds. How will they cross the river?

Solution: Dan and Dave go first. Dan

comes back and the father rows over by himself. Dave returns to pick up Dan.

Teaser: You have a job delivering pizzas for a restaurant. The restaurant requires a pizza to be delivered every half hour. How long will it take you to deliver three pizzas?

Answer: One hour. Make the first delivery at 10:00 AM, and the second one at 10:30. The third will be at 11:00, exactly one hour later.

What state is round at both ends and high in the middle?
Ohio.

Problem: A kid comes home from school each afternoon to the high-rise apartment building where he lives. Some days, he gets off the elevator at the eighth floor and walks up four flights, to his family's apartment on the twelfth floor. On other days he goes right up to the twelfth floor. Why?

Solution: He's too short to reach past the eighth floor button. So unless someone else is on the elevator with him, he must get off at the eighth floor.

I am you uncle's sister but I'm not your aunt. Who am I?

Your mother.

Puzzle: A farmer is served two freshly laid eggs for breakfast every morning. He does not own any chickens. He does not buy or steal the eggs. He does not trade for them or find them, and no one gives them to him. Where does the farmer get his eggs?

Answer: From ducks.

In what way are a napkin and an elephant alike?

Both are hard to keep on your lap.

Teaser: Take your age, and multiply it by two. Add five. Multiply by fifty. Subtract three-hundred-and-sixty-five. Add the loose change in your pocket under a dollar. Add one-hundred-fifteen. The first two figures in the answer are your age, and the last two the change in your pocket.

When does Thursday come before Wednesday?

Only in the dictionary.

Problem: In the Smith family there are seven sisters, and each sister has one brother. Including Mr. and Mrs. Smith, how many in the family?

Solution: Ten—both parents, the seven daughters and just one brother.

Puzzle: If the Vice-President of the United States should die, who would be President?

Answer: The President.

Puzzle: How many times can you subtract 2 from 21?

Answer: Only once. From then on, you would be subtracting from 19, then 17 and then from 15 and so forth.

Problem: Would it be cheaper for you to take one friend to the movies twice or two friends at the same time?

Solution: Two friends at the same time. Then you would have to buy only three tickets. If you took one friend twice, you would have to buy his ticket twice and your own twice. That would be four tickets.

Problem: When you take two apples from three apples, what do you have?

Solution: You have the two apples that you took.

Puzzle: I am the sister-in-law of your father's only brother. Who am I?

Answer: Your mother.

Puzzle: This can be repeated only once. *(Read it slowly.)* The bus has six passengers after you get on. It proceeds a few blocks and stops. Two passengers get off and five get on. It continues several blocks and stops. Three get off and seven board. It starts again, continues, then stops and four get off and four get on. It proceeds on its route, stops and five get on, three leave, then two more get on. On the next stop, 14 get on and no one gets off. How many stops did it make?

Answer: Gotcha! You were counting the number of people remaining on the bus probably. It made five stops.

Puzzle: I can run but I can't walk. What am I?

Answer: Water.

Puzzle: How can you drop an egg three feet without breaking it?

Answer: Hold the egg four feet above the floor. Let it drop three feet and then catch it.

Problem: Can you put your left hand deep into your right-hand pants pocket and your right hand deep into your left-hand pants pocket both at the same time? How?

Solution: Put your pants on backward.

Name the capital of every state in four seconds.

Washington, D.C.

Puzzle: If you drop a steel ball, would it fall more rapidly through water at twenty degrees or water at sixty degrees?

Answer: Sixty degrees. Water at twenty degrees would be ice.

Five boys *(Tom, Dick, Harry, Mike, and Joe)* met at the local fast-food restaurant. Tom, Dick, Harry, and Mike each ordered cokes at ten cents each. Dick had an extra coke and a piece of pie which cost sixty cents. Tax on the entire bill was four cents.

When the waitress brought the check, she had jotted down the figures:

80

20

10

10

4

"She didn't add it," said Tom. "So who pays what?"

"That's easy," said Joe. "Dick pays the top figure. Tom the second; Harry the third; and Mike the fourth. You split the fifth figure four ways. Put all nine figures together properly, and that's what I pay."

Can you arrange the nine figures to show what Joe had in mind?

Answer: Arrange the nine figures this way:

1 0 2 0 0 4 1 8 0

(I ought to owe nothing for I ate nothing.)

School Jokes

Teacher: How would you punctuate this sentence? "I saw a five dollar bill on the sidewalk."

Student: I would make a dash after it!

"I understand," said the teacher to the phone caller. "You say Jeff has a bad cold and won't be able to attend school today. And who is this speaking?"

"Why this," said the brusque voice, "is my father."

SUBSTITUTE TEACHER: How did the first American barbers arrive?

STUDENT: On clipper ships.

How do you spell dog backward?
D-o-g b-a-c-k-w-a-r-d!

TEACHER: Which is farther away, South Africa or the moon?

STUDENT: South Africa.

TEACHER: What makes you think that?

STUDENT: We can see the moon, but we can't see South Africa.

TEACHER: What made Francis Scott Key famous?

RYAN: He was the only person in history who knew all of the verses of "The Star-Spangled Banner."

"Which travels faster, heat or cold?" asked the science teacher.

"Heat," answered the student. "Anybody can catch a cold!"

"Tell me what you know about George Washington," asked the teacher.

"Well," replied the student, "I know he wasn't too smart."

"What makes you say that about the father of our country?"

"Well, I saw a picture of him crossing the Delaware, and everybody knows it's not too smart to stand up in a rowboat."

TEACHER: What travels around the earth without using a single drop of fuel?

STUDENT: The moon.

The teacher asked his students to write a composition titled "What I want to be when I grow up."

After the papers were passed in, he called Joel to his desk.

"It says here that you want to be the first person to land on the sun. Don't you know you'd burn to pieces?"

"Well, Sir, I was planning to go at night."

TEACHER: Tell me, Ben, did you ever see the Catskill Mountains?

BEN: No, Sir, I haven't, but I've seen them kill mice!

MOTHER: Everything is going up these days! Food, clothing, gasoline, I just wish one thing would go down!

JANE: Your wish has come true. Take a look at my report card.

TEACHER: What did a digital clock say to its mother?

STUDENT: Look, Ma! No hands!

"Our discussion today," said the teacher, "will be on lying. How many of you read chapter 18?"

Almost everyone in the class raised their hand.

"Then lying is the perfect subject for today since our textbook has only 17 chapters."

TEACHER: Why was George Washington buried at Mount Vernon?

STUDENT: Because he was dead.

GENE: How was the first grade today, Steve?

STEVE: It was fun. Tomorrow I have to take a holster and a toy gun.

GENE: For Show and Tell?

STEVE: No. Teacher said tomorrow she's going to teach us to draw!

TEACHER: Yes, Rod, what is it?

ROD: I don't want to scare you, but my Dad says if I don't start getting better grades, somebody's cruisin' for a bruisin!

What's the difference between a computer and a classroom teacher?

Computers can't give dirty looks.

TEACHER: Class, we have learned that the former ruler of Russia was called a czar and his wife was known as the czarina. What did they call their children?

GIRL: Czardines!

Ten-year-old Brad was asked by his teacher to name the four seasons of the year.

His answer? "Football, basketball, baseball, and vacation."

SON: Mom, the teacher got mad at me today because I didn't know where North Dakota was.

MOTHER: Well, Son, I've told you a million times, if you put things away, you'd know where to find them!

Why won't computers ever replace books?

There's no place to put the bookmark.

The class had just finished their science lesson for the day.

"Jessica," said the teacher, "what is the most important thing we learned about chemistry?"

Jessica lifted her head off the desk and answered weakly, "Never lick the spoon."

TEACHER: Ashley, can you give me Lincoln's Gettysburg Address?

ASHLEY: No, but he used to live at the White House in Washington, D.C.

TEACHER: Andi, what is cleanliness next to?

ANDI: Impossible.

What are the three most-used words in school?

Answer: I don't know.

A teacher's conference on communication was opened with the question, "What were Alexander Graham Bell's famous first words?"

Goo-goo.

"Bobby," asked a teacher, "if I lay one egg on the table and two on the chair, how many will I have altogether?"

"Personally," answered Bobby, "I don't think you can do it."

The teacher was giving a lesson on good manners. "With which hand do we stir our tea?"

Michael raised his hand and spoke quite snappily, "One should always use their right hand."

"No, Sir," said Justin. "You should always use a spoon."

Who can speak in all languages?
An echo.

MATTHEW: Do you think it's possible to predict the future?

MELINDA: Mom can. She takes one look at my report card and tells me exactly what Dad is going to do when he gets home.

TEACHER: There will be an eclipse of the moon tonight. Perhaps your parents will let you stay up and watch it.

PUPIL: What channel will it be on?

The teacher was trying to get his class to write a composition on a subject they all liked. Since most of the kids liked sports, he asked each of them to write a paper on baseball.

When the papers were handed in, the teacher was pleased with all but one paper. One student had written a composition on a baseball in just three words: "Game rained out."

"This is a sticky situation," said the teacher when she upset the rubber cement.

Lisa was talking on the phone to her friend Judy.

"First I got laryngitis, then tonsillitis and pneumonia, next I got hemophilia and I ended up getting hypodermics and inoculations!" moaned Lisa.

"Boy!" said Judy. "You sure have had a rough time!"

"I'll say! I thought I'd never get through that spelling contest!"

Why are fish so smart?
They travel in schools.

BRANDON: Today on the school bus a little boy fell off his seat, and everybody laughed except me.

TEACHER: Who was the little boy?

BRANDON: Me.

TEACHER: Class, we've learned that heat makes objects expand and cold makes them contract. John, would you give us an example?

JOHN: Yeah, in the summer when it's hot the days are longer. In the winter when it's cold, the days get shorter.

What is the difference between an engineer and a schoolteacher?

One minds the train—the other trains the mind.

TEACHER: What month has twenty-eight days?

STUDENT: All of them.

"Now, David, aren't you ashamed for having forgotten your pen? What would you call a soldier who went to battle without a gun?"

"A general," piped David.

TEACHER: What great event took place in 1809?

LESLIE: Lincoln was born.

TEACHER: Correct. Now someone tell me what happened in 1812.

LESLIE: Yes, Teacher, Lincoln had his third birthday.

TEACHER: Trevor, your composition describing your home is the same as your sister's—word for word.

TREVOR: Well, it's the same house.

TEACHER: *(rapping on desk):* Order, please.

SLEEPY VOICE FROM REAR: Cheeseburger, no onions for me.

TEACHER: Melonie, name two pronouns.

MELONIE: Who, me?

TEACHER: That's correct.

TEACHER: Students, there will be only a half day of school this morning.

STUDENTS: Whoopee! Hooray! Hippee!

TEACHER: Silence. We will have the other half this afternoon.

TEACHER: Were the questions on the test hard?

STUDENT: Oh, the questions were easy. It was the answers I had trouble with.

TEACHER: Tell me, Son. What are your dreams about?

PHILLIP: I dream about baseball.

TEACHER: Don't you ever dream about anything else?

PHILLIP: Nope. Just baseball.

TEACHER: Don't you ever dream about girls?

PHILLIP: What? And miss my turn at bat?

Silly Questions

How can three kids go out under only one umbrella and not get wet?
It isn't raining.

What Roman numeral climbs the wall?
IV (Ivy).

What did the big toe say to the little toe?
"Don't look now, but there's a heel following us."

What word has the most letters in it?
Mailbox.

What do you lose every time you stand up?
Your lap.

What do you call a happy lassie?
A jolly collie!

Why does a fireman wear red suspenders?
To hold up his pants.

How do you stop a 200-pound gerbil from charging?
Take away his credit cards!

Where was the Declaration of Independence signed?
At the bottom.

Why did the rocket lose it's job?
It got fired!

Why did the little girl throw the clock out the window?
She wanted to watch time fly.

Why do birds always fly south?
Because it's too far to walk.

What is the best way to make a fire with two sticks?

Be sure one of the sticks is a match.

What is the best thing to take when you are rundown?

The license plate of the car that hit you.

What goes up when the rain comes down?

Umbrellas.

What's a good pet for a conceited actor?

A hamster!

What animal can jump higher than a house?

All animals. Houses can not jump.

What is an important aid in good grooming for pet mice?

Mousewash!

What is an eagle after he is five days old?

Six days old.

Question: Four men fell into the water but only three of them got their hair wet.
Answer: One of them was bald.

What is the first thing you put in a garden?
Your foot!

What's better than a talking parrot?
A spelling bee.

What is the smallest room known to man?
A mushroom.

What dog keeps the best time?
A watchdog.

What beans do not grow in a garden?
Jelly beans.

FIRST METER READER: A dog bit me on the leg this morning!

SECOND METER READER: Did you put anything on it?

FIRST METER READER: No, he liked it plain!

Where does a sheep get his hair cut?
At the baa-baa shop.

What are the strongest creatures in the ocean?
Mussels.

If you were locked in a room that had in it only a bed and a calendar, what would you eat?
Water from the bed springs and dates from the calendar.

What is big and blue and eats rocks?
A big blue rock eater.

Where do computers keep their valuables?
In data banks.

How many balls of string would it take to reach Mars?
Just one. But it would have to be a very big one.

If all the cars in America were white, what would we have?

A white car nation.

Why do elephants float down the river on their backs?

So they won't get their tennis shoes wet.

What is the hardest thing about riding a skateboard?

The pavement.

Why does a hen lay eggs?

If she let them drop, they would break.

What do they call cabs lined up at Texas airports?

The yellow rows of taxis.

Which pets always lie around the house?

Carpets!

What are the largest diamonds in the United States?

Baseball fields.

What can make more noise than a kitten stuck in a tree?

Two kittens stuck in a tree.

Where can you go to always find money?
The dictionary.

Two young passengers on the city bus.

"Excuse me, does this bus stop at Main Street?"

"Yes, just watch me and get off one stop before me."

Why is a dirty kid like a new pair of jeans?

They both shrink from washing.

Why does a baby pig eat so much?
To make a hog of himself.

What kind of shoes are never out of style at gas stations?

Pumps.

Which pet is a librarian's best friend?
The catalog!

If a man is born in Tasmania, grows up in Bulgaria, moves to Mexico, and dies in New York City, what is he?

Dead.

If you drop a white hat into the Red Sea, what will it become?

Wet.

What do you call a man who's always wiring for money?

An electrician.

Why does a stork stand on one leg?

Because if he took both legs off the ground, he would fall down.

Name six things that have milk in them.

Butter, cheese, ice cream, and three cows.

What did the mayonnaise say to the refrigerator?

"Close the door, I'm dressing."

When is a cook bad?

When she beats an egg and whips the cream.

How do they put the milk in the Milky Way?

With the Big Dipper!

Question: On which side of a cat do you find the most fur?

Answer: The outside.

What does a cowgirl say at the end of a long ride?

Whoa!

What kind of weather pleases a pet duck?

Fowl weather!

What does Santa say when he works in his garden?

Hoe, Hoe, Hoe!

What did the carpenter say to the wall?

"One more crack like that and I'll plaster you."

What do birds say on Halloween?
Trick or tweet.

What is brown, has a hump, and lives at the North Pole?
Rudolph the Red-nosed Camel.

Where are kings usually crowned?
On the head.

How do you stop a five-pound parrot from talking too much?
Get a ten-pound cat!

What is the difference between a counterfeit ten-dollar bill and an angry rabbit?
One is bad money and the other is a mad bunny.

What highly valued pet can you find at a variety store?
A goldfish!

FIVE-YEAR-OLD: I wonder what thumbs are for?
SEVEN-YEAR-OLD: They're to hold up bottoms of sandwiches.

What did the boy say when he saw his dog lying in the sun?

Hot dog!

Why did the dog keep chasing his tail?

He wanted to see if he could make ends meet!

What kind of turtle must you never trust?

A turtle-tale!

"Are you a little boy or a little girl?"

"Sure, what else could I be?"

Question: What kind of a dog will you bite?

Answer: A hot dog!

"Ask me if I'm a rabbit."

"OK, are you a rabbit?"

"Yes, I'm a rabbit. Now ask me if I'm an alligator."

"I'm game. Are you an alligator?"

"No, you dummy, I told you I'm a rabbit!"

How are dogs and trees alike?
One barks and the other has bark.

What has the head of a cat, the tail of a cat, and the ways of a cat, but isn't a cat?
A kitten!

If King Midas sat on a pile of gold, who sat on silver?
The Lone Ranger!

How do you tell an elephant from a banana?
A banana is yellow.

What did Tarzan say when he saw the lions coming?
"There come the lions."

What did Tarzan say when he saw the elephants coming, "There come the elephants?"
No, he said, "There comes the bananas."
He was color blind!

Joel: What would you do if you were in my shoes?
Patrick: I'd polish them!

Question: What is cowhide used for?
Answer: To hold the cow together.

Why did the baby strawberry cry?
Because her mother was in a jam.

What animal always goes to bed with his shoes on?
A horse.

What three keys won't open doors?
Monkeys, donkeys, and turkeys.

What did the "daddy" firecracker say to the "baby" firecracker?
My pop's bigger than your pop.

If the red house is on the right and the blue house is on the left, where is the white house?
In Washington, D.C.

What did Frankenstein say when the electricity went off?

A.C. come, A.C. go.

What is it that is always coming but never arrives?

Tomorrow. When it arrives, it is today.

How many letters are there in the alphabet.

Eleven: t-h-e a-l-p-h-a-b-e-t.

What is the difference between an old penny and a new nickel?

Four cents.

Some people say that I have a head and a tail, but no body. What am I?

A penny.

What looks like an elephant and flies?

A flying elephant.

What is the best way to double your money?

Fold it!

What is the very last thing you take off when you go to bed?

Your feet off the floor.

Question: What's the difference between an elephant and a mouse?

Answer: About 5,000 pounds.

I have four legs and only one foot. What am I?

A bed.

What does a worm do in a cornfield?

He goes in one ear and out the other.

What do a clock and a river have in common?

Neither will run without winding.

Why don't more elephants go to college?

Not too many elephants finish high school.

What is the best way to prevent infection from biting insects?

Stop biting them.

What word is always pronounced wrong?
"Wrong."

When was beef the highest?
When the cow jumped over the moon.

What has an eye but sees nothing?
A needle.

How do you put six elephants in a Volkswagen?
Three in the front seat and three in the backseat.

What has cities but no houses, parks but no people, and lakes but no water?
A map.

What does the wisest person overlook?
His nose.

Question: Why do hummingbirds hum?
Answer: Because they don't know the words!

How is an island like the letter T?
Both are in the middle of water.

What has two feet on either side and one in the middle?
A yardstick.

What goes ninety-nine thump, ninety-nine thump, ninety-nine thump?
A centipede with a wooden leg.

Why do elephants have flat feet?
From jumping out of trees.

Why is a dentist unhappy at work?
Because he is always looking down in the mouth.

Which American President wore the largest hat?
The one with the biggest head.

Define a volcano?
A mountain with the hiccups.

How do you know when an elephant is in a telephone booth with you?

You can smell the peanuts on his breath.

What did the big rose say to the little rose?

Hello, Bud!

What time is it when a clock strikes thirteen times?

Time to get a new clock.

Why is the Ohio River so rich?

It has two banks of its own.

How does an elephant put his trunk in a crocodile's mouth?

Very carefully.

What question can never be answered by yes?

Are you asleep?

What do you call elephants who ride on trains?

Passengers.

What letter cannot be found in the alphabet?

The one the postman delivers.

What is the difference between here and there?

Only the letter T.

How can you tell if an elephant's been in the refrigerator?

He leaves footprints in the butter.

What is worse than a giraffe with a sore throat?

A centipede with athlete's foot.

What did George Washington say to his men just before they got in the boat?

"Get in the boat!"

What does every duck become the first time it takes to water?

A wet duck.

Where do you find elephants?

Where you lose them.

What has eighteen legs and sometimes catches flies.

A baseball team.

What gets wetter and wetter the more it dries?

A towel.

JEFF: Doctor, will I be able to read with these glasses?

DOCTOR: Yes.

JEFF: Great! I've never read before.

What did the elephant say when the Volkswagen ran into it?

"How many times have I told you kids not to play in the street?"

What must you keep after giving it to someone else?

Your word.

How do you know when you're no longer wanted?

They remove your picture at the post office.

How does an elephant get out of a phone booth?

The same way he got in.

POLICEMAN: Little fellow, why do you keep going around the block?

LITTLE FELLOW: I'm running away from home, but I'm not allowed to cross the street by myself.

What building has the most stories?

The public library.

What has neither flesh nor bones but has four fingers and a thumb?

A baseball glove.

How can you tell when an elephant is getting ready to charge?

He takes out his credit card.

What do you call a rabbit with lots of fleas?

Bugs Bunny.

What begins with *E* and ends with *E* and has a letter in between?

An envelope.

What do you do when an elephant sneezes?

Run!

To whom does everyone take off his hat?

The barber.

How many big men have been born in Ohio?

None. Only small babies.

What do you call a hippopotamus who's been carrying elephants across the river all day?

A tired hippo.

What runs up to your house but never goes in?

The sidewalk.

What happens to a black cow when it stands out in the rain?

It gets wet.

What did the banana say to the elephant?

Nothing, bananas don't talk. They just stalk.

Where were Sally's friends when the lights went out?

In the dark.

What did the baby porcupine say to the cactus?

Are you my mother?

What do you call a man who shaves ten times a day?

A barber.

What three-letter word is a mousetrap?

Cat.

What is the best month for a parade?

March.

What goes clomp, clomp, clomp, clomp, clomp, clomp, clomp, squoosh?

An octopus with one shoe off.

Did you ever see . . .
    A horse fly?
    A pen point?
    A clock strike?
    A window box?
    A rabbit punch?
    A jelly roll?
    A fish bowl?
    A barn dance?
    A clam bake?
    A banana peel?
    A tooth brush?
    A ski jump?

Animal Jokes

Why did the mama flea look so sad?
Because all her children were going to the dogs.

What dogs are best for sending telegrams?
Wire-haired terriers.

JENNIE: I've got a cat who can say its own name!
MATTHEW: That's great! What's your cat's name?
JENNIE: Meow.

What dog stands the best chance of winning the heavyweight title?
A boxer.

TURTLE #1: I want to get a gift for my wife for her birthday. Got any suggestions?

TURTLE #2: How about a people-neck sweater?

TRACIE: Why do you think ants are so smart?

DAVID: Because they always seem to know when we're having a picnic.

LOYD: What do you feed your pet frog?

KEITH: Croakers and milk!

Tommy, the leopard, stopped to see an optometrist about a problem.

"Every time I look at my best friend, I see spots before my eyes," he said.

"What do you expect?" answered the optometrist. "You're a leopard, aren't you?"

"Yes," replied Tommy, "but my best friend is a zebra."

When can you take your pet rabbit to a dance?

When it's a bunny hop!

BILLY: I taught my dog to play checkers.

SAM: You must have a pretty smart dog.

BILLY: Not that smart. I can beat him two out of three games!

A brilliant magician was performing on an ocean liner. But every time he did a trick, a talking parrot in the audience would scream, "It's a trick. It's not magic. He's a big phony!"

One night during a storm, the ship sank while the magician was performing. And who should end up in the same lifeboat together, all alone, but the talking parrot and the magician!

For three days, they glared at each other, neither one saying a word to the other.

Finally the parrot sighed and said, "All right, smart aleck, you and your stupid tricks. What did you do with the ship?"

A mother skunk was worried because she had trouble keeping track of her two children. They were named In and Out. And whenever In was in, Out was out. But if Out was in, then In was out.

One day the mother skunk called Out in to her and told him to go out and bring In in. So Out went out and, in no time at all, brought In in.

"Wonderful!" said the mother skunk. "How, in all this great forest, could you find In in so short a time?"

"It was easy," said Out. "Instinct."

Which part of a fish weighs the most? The scales!

A housewife walked into a fish market, peered into the case and said, "I don't like the looks of that fish."

"Well, lady," stated the clerk, "by the way he's eyeing you, he doesn't like your looks, either."

Question: Why does your pet owl go "Tweet, tweet" instead of "hoot" like other owls?

Answer: Because he doesn't give a hoot!

MOTHER: Rusty, eat those carrots. They are good for your eyesight.

RUSTY: How do you know, Mom?

MOTHER: Did you ever see a rabbit with glasses?

"Doctor, Doctor, you've got to help my brother! He thinks he's a dog!"

"How long has this been going on?"

"Ever since he was a pup!"

FATHER KANGAROO: Good grief! Where is the baby?

MOTHER KANGAROO: Oh, no! My pocket's been picked!

What is the difference between a cat and a comma?

One means "pause at the end of a clause" and the other means "claws at the end of paws!"

BABY OCTOPUS: Mommy, will you help me put my tennis shoes on?

MOTHER OCTOPUS: Good grief! I only have eight hands!

The telephone on the desk of a reporter for a large city newspaper rang many, many times.

He picked it up and a voice said, "You're all wet about the high cost of living. My wife and I live real good, eating everything we like, on less than two dollars a week."

"Two dollars a week!" cried the reporter. "I can't believe it! Please tell me how you do it and, to make sure I get the story straight, please speak louder."

"I can't speak louder," came the answer. "I'm a goldfish."

What did the sardine say when he swam past the submarine?

"Look! A can of people!"

How can you tell if your cat can count?

Ask it what one minus one is, then see if the cat says nothing!

MOTHER: Did you change the water in the goldfish bowl?

DAUGHTER: No, Mom, they didn't drink what I gave them yesterday.

Two fleas came out of a movie. It was raining. One flea said to the other, "Do you want to walk home, or should we take a dog?"

What is worse than an elephant with a cold in its nose?
A centipede with sore feet!

Where do dogs like to keep their cars?
In a barking lot!

An earthworm and a snail decided to take a trip. When they arrived at the airport, there were only two seats left—one aboard a plane and one aboard a helicopter.

"You take the plane," said the snail, "and I'll go by helicopter."

"Absolutely not!" said the earthworm.

"I do not see what difference it makes," grumbled the snail.

"Plenty," replied the earthworm. "The whirlybird always gets the worm."

BEVERLY: What is the highest award a cat can earn?
THEO: The Purr-litzer prize.

FARMER: That kid visiting our son is really a city boy.

WIFE: Why do you say that?

FARMER: He saw some milk bottles behind the barn and ran to me shouting he'd found a cow's nest.

AL: Did you know it takes ten mink to make one jacket?

YOUTH: I didn't even know they could sew!

A teenager was sitting in a movie behind a friend and his dog. During the happy scenes the dog wagged his tail. During the sad scenes the dog whimpered. When the villain appeared, the dog growled. During the kissing scenes the dog put his paws over his eyes.

When the movie ended, the teenager said to his friend, "I can't believe your dog! I have never seen a dog react like that to a movie!"

"That's nothing," replied the friend. "You should have seen him when he read the book!"

AUNT: Why are you crying?

NIECE: Because I wanted to get a dog for my new baby brother.

AUNT: Well, that's no reason to cry.

NIECE: Yes it is! Nobody would trade with me!

FREDA: Doctor, Doctor, please come over right away. My dog swallowed a fountain pen!

DOCTOR: I'll be right there, but what are you doing in the meantime?

FREDA: I'm using a pencil.

TOM: I saw a baby today that gained twenty pounds in one week by drinking elephant's milk.

ANN: Amazing! Whose baby was it?

TOM: The elephant's!

LAURA: I've got an alligator named Ginger.

BRIAN: Does Ginger bite?

LAURA: No, Ginger snaps.

MOTHER OWL: I'm worried about Ronnie.

FATHER OWL: What's the matter?

MOTHER OWL: Well, he doesn't give a hoot about anything.

A farmer's wife opened her refrigerator and found a rabbit inside, "What are you doing here?" she asked.

"Isn't this a Westinghouse?" asked the rabbit.

The woman said, "Yes."

"Well, I'm westing," replied the rabbit.

A gorilla walked into a drugstore, ordered a $1.00 sundae, and put down a ten-dollar bill to pay for it. The clever clerk thought "Gorillas don't know much about money," and handed him a five dollar bill.

The clerk's curiosity got the best of him and he said, "We don't get too many gorillas in here."

"No wonder," the gorilla replied, "at five dollars a sundae."

EYE DOCTOR: What seems to be the trouble?

ZEBRA TRAINER: "I don't know. I keep seeing stripes before my eyes!"

A cowboy, while riding his horse, saw a small dog running down the road.

"Hi," said the small dog.

"Hi," said the cowboy.

A few moments later the cowboy said out loud, "That's funny. I didn't know dogs could talk!"

The horse turned his head, looked at the cowboy, and said, "You learn something new every day."

Do you know how to sculpture a horse?

Sure. Just take a big block of marble and chip away anything that doesn't look like a horse.

What do you call a cat that digs in the sand?

Sandy Claws!

CHUCK: A bear ran through our camp last week, and our camp leader shot the bear in his pajamas.

SHERRI: Don't kid me. Bears don't wear pajamas!

What do you call a duck that makes straight *A*'s on his report card?

A wise quacker.

MIKE: Did I ever tell you about the time I came face to face with a tiger?

LORI: No, what happened?

MIKE: There I stood without a gun, while the tiger growled and crawled closer and closer.

LORI: What did you do?

MIKE: I moved on to the next cage!

When do horses have sixteen feet?

When there are four horses.

SNAKE #1: I sure hope I'm not poisonous!

SNAKE #2: Why?

SNAKE #1: Because I just bit my tongue!

What do you call it when a cat shows good manners?

Eti-cat, of course!

Why did the elephant sit on the marshmallow?

So he wouldn't fall into the hot chocolate.

LITTLE BOY: I'd like some birdseed, please.

PET SHOP OWNER: How many birds do you have?

LITTLE BOY: None! I want to grow some!

Why do elephants wear pink tennis shoes?

Because white ones get dirty too fast.

MOTHER LION: Junior, what are you doing?

BABY LION: I'm chasing a hunter around a tree.

MOTHER LION: How many times have I told you not to play with your food?

MIKE: I can't talk to you while my goat is nearby.

TOM: Why not?

MIKE: Because he always butts in!

What do giraffes have that no other animals have?

Baby giraffes.

DAD: Andi, why are you crying?

ANDI: I cleaned the bird cage and the canary disappeared.

DAD: How did you clean it?

ANDI: With the vacuum cleaner.

What time is it when an elephant sits on a fence?

It's time to get a new fence.

JASON: If I say, "Come here, Buffy," will your dog come to me?

MARK: Nope.

JASON: Why not?

MARK: Because his name's Rover!

Which kind of dog is as warm as a blanket?

An Afghan!

Why does a giraffe eat so little?

A little goes a long way.

If twenty dogs run after one cat, what time is it?

Twenty after one.

A fish probably goes home and lies about the size of the bait he stole.

JOSHUA: My parents just bought me a bird for a pet.
KEITH: What kind is it?
JOSHUA: A keet.
KEITH: You mean a parakeet.
JOSHUA: No, they only bought me one.

The way most fishermen catch fish is by the tale!

What did the pig say when the farmer got him by the tail?
"This is the end of me!"

Question: What does a rabbit use to comb its fur?
Answer: A harebrush!

Why do elephants need trunks?
Because they don't have glove compartments.

When are mice and rats unhappy?
When it's raining cats and dogs!

Good Advice: When eating an elephant, take one bite at a time.

DAN: How does a whale cry?
DAVE: I don't know. How?
DAN: Blubber, blubber, blubber.

A duck walked into a store and said to a clerk, "I'd like some lipstick please."

The clerk was surprised at the duck's request, but he got the lipstick, handed it to the duck and said, "That's $2.98."

The duck replied, "Oh, just put it on my bill!"

Brother and Sister Jokes

Why did your brother go to night school?
Because he wanted to learn to read in the dark.

Did you hear about my sister? She saw a moose's head hanging on a wall and went into the next room to see the rest of it.

Why did your sister put a chicken in a tub of hot water?
Because she wanted the chicken to lay hard-boiled eggs.

BIG BROTHER: That planet over there is Mars.

LITTLE SISTER: Then that other must be Pa's.

Why did your brother empty his watch on the tomato pie?

Because he wanted a pizza with the works!

Why did your sister cut a hole in her new umbrella?

Because she wanted to be able to tell when it stopped raining.

Why did your brother shoot the alarm clock?

Because he felt like killing time.

Why did your computer get arrested?

Because it was robbing the memory bank.

Did you hear about the sister who wrote herself a letter and forgot to sign it, and when it arrived she didn't know who it was from?

Why did your brother separate the thread from the needle?

Because the needle had something in its eye.

Why did your brother run through a screen door?

Because he wanted to strain himself.

Why did your brother wear a wet shirt all day?

Because the label said, "Wash and wear."

Why did your brother spend two weeks in a revolving door?

Because he was looking for the doorknob.

Why did your sister order artificial water?

Because someone sent her artificial flowers!

Why was your brother fired from his job as an elevator operator?

Because he couldn't remember the route.

Why did your brother jump out the window?

Because he wanted to try out his new spring suit!

Why did your brother refuse the gift of a Japanese car?

Because he'd never be able to learn the language!

Why did your sister drink the cleaning fluid?

Because she wanted to get rid of the spots before her eyes!

Did you hear about the boy that got his sister a birthday cake, but could not figure out how to get the cake in the typewriter to write "Happy Birthday?"

Why did your brother plant birdseed?

Because he wanted to raise canaries.

Why does your brother wear a life jacket to bed?

Because he sleeps on a waterbed!

Why did your sister ask her father to sit in the refrigerator?

Because she wanted ice cold pop!

Why did your brother refuse to accept tickets for a door prize?

Because he already had a door!

Why did your brother tiptoe past the medicine cabinet?

Because he didn't want to wake the sleeping pills.

BROTHER: If you broke your arm in two places, what would you do?

SISTER: I wouldn't go back to those two places.

Why does your sister jump up and down before taking her medicine?

Because the label said, "Shake well before using."

BROTHER: Did you know that it takes three sheep to make a sweater?

SISTER: No, I didn't even know they could knit.

Why did your brother give cough syrup to the pony?

Because someone told him it was a little horse.

BROTHER: How do you top a car?
SISTER: Tep on the brake, tupid.

Why does your brother have yeast and shoe polish for breakfast?
Because he wants to rise and shine!

BROTHER: "Did you just take a shower?"
SISTER: "Why, is one missing?"

Why does your brother keep running around his bed?
Because he was trying to catch up with his sleep.

BROTHER: Why is the dog staring at me like that?'
SISTER: Don't mind him. He's just mad 'cause you're eating out of his dish!

Why does your brother put his socks on inside out?
Because there was a hole on the outside.

BROTHER: What two things can you never eat for breakfast?
SISTER: Lunch and dinner.

Why did your brother take a bicycle to bed?

Because he didn't want to walk in his sleep.

BROTHER: What happened to you?
SISTER: I fell while I was riding.
BROTHER: Horseback?
SISTER: I don't know. I'll find out when I get back to the barn!

Why does your brother pick up soap bubbles and put them to his ear?

Because he likes soap operas.

SISTER: Why are you putting the saddle on backwards?
BROTHER: How do you know which way I'm going?

Why did your brother pitch the tent on top of the stove?

Because he wanted a home on the range!

BROTHER: Did you put the cat out?
SISTER: Why, is it on fire?

Why does your sister dislike peanuts?
Has anyone ever seen a skinny elephant?

BROTHER: What kind of sharks never eat women?
SISTER: Man-eating sharks!

Why did your brother feed money to his cow?
Because he wanted to get rich milk.

BROTHER: Where was Solomon's temple?
SISTER: On either side of his head.

Why couldn't your brother spell Mississippi when the teacher asked him?
Because he didn't know if she meant the river or the state!

BROTHER: Is it true that bears will not hurt you if you carry a slingshot?
SISTER: It depends on how "fast" you carry it!

Why does your brother want to buy a sea horse?

Because he wants to play water polo!

BROTHER: What goes up but never comes down?

SISTER: My age!